She Said It

A collection of quotes by remarkable women

Curated by Diane Darling

Special edition for

As a little one, it was easy to figure out what my carpenter grandfather did. I couldn't figure out what my lawyer grandfather did.

One day I mustered the courage to ask.

He paused for what seemed like an eternity. Then he said, "I ask people to honor the Ten Commandments."

That was my introduction to the legal world.

Congratulations to the Center for Women in Law and all you do.

Introduction

As a speaker I see many talks. Often, they start with a quote.

I started noticing how rarely the quotes were by women. So, I put together this book because I was tired of seeing women speak at events and have quotes from only men.

Don't get me wrong. Men have said some amazing things. However so have women.

Names and not titles – I decided not to include the title (e.g. author, activist, CEO) next to the person's name. I wanted their words rather than their title stand out. If you have a smart speaker (e.g. Alexa), spend some time asking her about these women.

If you have some favorite quotes you would like included in the future, please email it to: Diane@DianeDarling.com and put book "Women Quote" in the subject line.

Hopefully this book of quotes will be one of many.

If you find a typo or error, my apologies and please do let me know so it can be corrected in future editions.

Look forward to hearing your feedback and getting your favorites to include in the future.

Warm regards,

Diane

Diane Darling
April 2019 – Boston, MA

Dedication

This book is dedicated to all the amazing women who have gone before me. Your courage, tenacity, and resilience are an inspiration every day.

Honorable mention to Ann Bardwell Darling who literally brought me into the world. I miss you dearly, your words guide me daily, and I try to honor your wisdom each and every moment.

A phrase I remember you telling me over and over again, "Diane, you're trying to do too much in too little time." Mom, I'm still a work-in-progress.

Now enjoy the following quotations.

Persistence is failing 19 times and succeeding the 20th. ~ Julie Andrews

Perhaps it is impossible for a person who does no good to do no harm. ~ Harriett Beecher Stowe

People think it's the end of the day a man is the only answer. Actually, a fulfilling job is better for me. ~ Princess Diana

When anyone tells me I can't do anything ... I'm just not listening anymore. ~ Florence Griffith Joyner

What difference does it make if the thing you were scared of is real or not? ~ Tony Morrison

We will be victorious if we have not forgotten how to learn. ~ Rosa Luxemburg

We must not allow other peoples limited perceptions to define us. ~ Virginia Satir

Today's business leader cannot justify her existence by profit statements alone. She must also render service to her local, national, and world community.
~ Dorothy Shaver

To love what you do and feel that it matters – how can anything be more fun?
~ Katherine Graham

To be or not to be is not a question of compromise. Either you be or you don't be. ~ Golda Meir

Time is a dressmaker specializing in alterations. ~ Faith Baldwin

They say getting thin is the best revenge. Success is much better. ~ Oprah Winfrey

There's no reason to repeat bad history.
~ Elinor Holmes Norton

There is always sunshine, only we must do our part; we must move into it.
~ Clara Louise Burnham

Take your work seriously, but never yourself. ~ Dame Margot Fonteyn

The best of us must sometimes eat our words. ~ J. K. Rowling

Take your victories, whatever they may be, cherish them, use them, but don't settle for them. ~ Mia Hamm

Succeeding in adversity makes success all the sweeter. At the end of the day, it's not how far you fall but how high you bounce. ~ Sheila Wellington

Study the rules so that you won't beat yourself by not knowing something. ~ Babe Didrikson Zaharias

If you want something done, ask a busy person to do it. The more things you do, the more you can do. ~ Lucille Ball

I feel confident that in the years ahead, many of the remaining outmoded barriers to women's aspirations will disappear. ~ Eleanor Roosevelt

If you want to thing done well, get a couple of older broads to do it. ~ Betty Davis

If you think you're too small to have an impact, try going to bed with a mosquito. ~ Anita Roddick

If you look at life one way, there is always cause for alarm. ~ Elizabeth Bowen

If you judge people, you have no time to love them. ~ Mother Teresa

If you have knowledge, let others light their candles in it. ~ Margaret Fuller

If you find it in your heart to care for somebody else, you will have succeeded. ~ Maya Angelou

If you feel like it's difficult to change, you will probably have a harder time succeeding. ~ Andrea Jung

If you do things well, do them better. Be daring, be first, be different, be just. ~ Anita Roddick

If we would build on a sure foundation in friendship, we would love our friends for their sake rather than our own. ~ Charlotte Brontë

If we don't change, we don't grow. If we don't grow, we aren't really living. ~ Gail Sheehy

If the world were logical place, men would ride side saddle. ~ Rita Mae Brown

Sometimes I feel discriminate against, but doesn't make me angry. It merely astonishes me. How can they deny themselves the pleasure of my company? It's beyond me. ~ Zora Neale Hurtson

The moment we began to fear the opinions of others and hesitate to tell the truth that is in us, and from motives of policy are silent when we should speak, the divine floods of light and life are no longer in our souls.
~ Elizabeth Cady Stanton

Philanthropy is not hazardous to corporate health. ~ Marilyn Carlson Nelson

Planning ahead is a measure of class.
~ Gloria Steinem

The longer we listen to one another – – with a real attention – – the more commonality we will find in all our lives. That is, if we are careful to exchange with one another life stories and not simply opinions. ~ Barbara Deming

The leadership instinct your bored with is the backbone. You develop a funny bone in a wishbone that go with it.
~ Elaine Agather

The kind of beauty I want most is the hard to get kind that comes from within – – strength, courage, dignity. ~ Ruby Dee

The imperative is to define what is right and do it. ~ Barbara Jordan

The first rule of a holes: when you're in one, stop digging. ~ Molly Ivins

The first problem for all of us, men and women, it's not to learn, but to unlearn. ~ Gloria Steinem

The essential conditions of everything you do my speech choice, love, passion. ~ Nadia Boulanger

Never underestimate the power of dreams and the influence of the human spirit. We are all the same in this notion. The potential for greatness lives with in each of us. ~ Wilma Rudolph

Never be afraid to sit a while and think. ~ Lorraine Hansberry

Write your thoughts here ….

My grandfather once told me that there were two kinds of people: those who do the work and those who take the credit. He told me to try and be in the first group; it was much less competition.
~ Indira Gandhi

My favorite thing is to go where I've never gone before. ~ Diane Arbus

Slaying the dragon of delay is no sports for the short-winded.
~ Sandra Day O'Connor

Self-reliance is the only road to freedom and being one's own person is the ultimate reward. ~ Patricia Sampson

People are more fun than anybody.
~ Dorothy Parker

Ordinary life does not interest me.
~ Anais Nin

One thing is clear to me: We, as human beings, must be willing to except people who are different from ourselves.
~ Barbara Jordan

One accurate measurement is worth a thousand expert opinions. ~ Grace Hopper

Of course there's no such thing as a totally objective person, except Almighty God, if she exists. ~ Antonia Fraser

Now maybe on career days a little girl can say she'd like to be a professional athlete. ~ Lisa Leslie

Nothing will work unless you do. ~ Maya Angelou

Nothing strengthens the judgment and quickens the conscious like individual responsibility. ~ Elizabeth Cady Stanton

Not everything that is faced can be changed, but nothing can be changed until it is faced. ~ Lucille Ball

It is our choices that show us who we are, far more than our abilities. ~ J. K. Rowling

It is of immense importance that we laugh at ourselves. ~ Katherine Mansfield

It is brave to be involved. To be not fearful to be unresolved. ~ Gwendolyn Brooks

It irritates me to be told how things have been done. I defy the tyranny of precedent. I cannot afford the luxury of a closed mind. I go for anything that might improve the past. ~ Clara Barton

Investments are made not in ideas, but in the people who can bring those ideas to life. ~ Dr. Myra Hart

Information voids will be filled by rumors and speculation until they are preempted by open, credible, and trustworthy communication. ~ Jean Keffeler

And every outthrust headland, and every curving beach, and every grain of sand there is a story of the earth.
~ Rachel Carlson

Normal is in the eye of the beholder.
~ Whoopi Goldberg

Nobody can be exactly like me. Sometimes even I have trouble doing it.
~ Tallulah Bankhead

No trumpet sound when the important decisions of our life are made. Destiny is made known silently ~ Agnes DeMille

No person is your friend for demands your silence, organize your right to grow.
~ Alice Walker

No one can argue any longer about the rights of women. It's like arguing about earthquakes. ~ Lillian Hellman

My address is like my shoes. It travels with me. I abide where there is a fight against wrong. ~ Mother Jones

Millions long for immortality who don't know what to do on a rainy afternoon.
~ Susan Ertz

Memories of our lives, our works and our deeds will continue in others.
~ Rosa Parks

Many persons have a wrong idea about what constitutes true happiness. It is not attained to self- gratification but through fidelity to a worthy purpose.
~ Helen Keller

Look at a day when you were supremely satisfied at the end. It's not a day when you lounge around doing nothing, it's when you've had everything to do and you've done it. ~ Margaret Thatcher

Listening, not intimidation, maybe the sincerest form of flattery.
~ Dr. Joyce Brothers

Like shrinks or expands according to one's courage. ~ Anais Nin

Life isn't a matter of milestones, but of moments. ~ Rose Fitzgerald Kennedy

Keep in mind always the present you are constructing. It should be the future you want. ~ Alice Walker

Justice is better than chivalry if we cannot have both. ~ Alice Stone Blackwell

Just trying to do something ~ just being there, showing up ~ is how we get braver. Self-esteem is about doing. ~ Joy Browne

Just go out there and do what you have to do. ~ Martina Navratilova

Just don't give up what you really want to do where there is love inspiration, I don't think you can go wrong. ~ Ella Fitzgerald

I've learned to make my mind large, as the universe is large, so there is no room for contradictions.
~ Maxine Hong Kingston

I've come to believe that each of us has a personal calling that's as unique as a fingerprint – and that the best way to succeed is discover what you love and then find a way to offer it to others in the form of service, working hard and also allowing the energy of the universe to lead you. ~ Oprah Winfrey

It's the moment you think you can't that you realize you can. ~ Celine Dion

It's not the load that breaks you down, it's the way you carry it. ~ Lena Horne

It's not a sacrifice if you love what you're doing. ~ Mia Hamm

It's better to look ahead and prepare them to look back and regret. ~ Jackie Joyner-Kersee

It took me a long time not to judge myself through someone else's eyes. ~ Sally Field

It occurred to me when I was 13 and wearing white gloves and Mary Janes and going to dancing school, that no one should have to dance backward all of their lives. ~ Jill Ruckelshaus

I believe love and work = health. Don't compromise on either one. ~ Bernadine Healy

Learning is nothing if not a messy process of discovery and unfolding. ~ Diana Chapman Walsh

I am my own woman. ~ Evita Peron

Good leadership is about the company's success, not your own. ~ Ann Mulcahy

Good enough never is. ~ Debbie Fields

It isn't where you came from, it's where you're going that counts. ~ Ella Fitzgerald

It is the mind that makes the body. ~ Sojourner Truth

I'm not afraid of storms, for I am learning to sail my ship. ~ Louisa May Alcott

If you want to make peace, you don't talk to your friends. You talk to your enemies. ~ Mother Teresa

If success is not on your own terms, if it looks good to the world but doesn't feel good in your heart, it is not success at all. ~ Anna Quindlen

List some people you would like to share a quote with ….

If one is rich and one's a woman, one can be quite misunderstood.
~ Katherine Graham

The need to die and be reborn, the need to be renewed, the need to encounter profoundly life's mystery, the need to engage the imagination – these arise for every living person. ~ Joan Halifax

If I don't have friends, then I ain't got nothing. ~ Billie Holiday

I was raised to believe that excellence is the best deterrent to racism or sexism. And that's how I operate in my life. ~ Oprah Winfrey

I wanted a perfect ending. Now I've learned, the hard way that some poems don't rhyme, and some stories don't have a clear beginning, middle, and end. Life is about not knowing, having to change, taking the moment and making the best, without knowing what's going to happen next. Delicious ambiguity. ~ Gilda Radner

I took a deep breath and listen to that all the bray of my heart. I am. I am. I am.
~ Sylvia Plath

I think the key for women is not to set any limits. ~ Martina Navratilova

I think that business practices would improve and measure live in measurably if they were guided by "feminine" principles – – qualities like love and care and intuition. ~ Anita Roddick

I suppose leadership at one time met muscles; but to gate means getting along with people. ~ Indira Gandhi

I realize that Huber isn't for everyone. It's only for people who want to have fun, enjoy life, and feel alive. ~ Ann Wilson Schaef

I never see what has been done; only see what remains to be done. ~ Maria Curie

I never ran my train off the track, and I never lost a passenger. ~ Harriet Tubman

To live a life in the spirit, to be true to a life in the spirit, we have to be willing to be called on - often in ways that we may not like. ~ Bell Hooks

I know God won't give me anything I can't handle. I just wish he didn't trust me so much. ~ Mother Teresa

I have no idea what Title IX is. Sorry.
~ Jennifer Capriati

I hate housework! You make the beds, you do the dishes, and six months later you have to start all over again! ~ Joan Rivers

I have never been especially impressed by the heroics of people convinced they are about to change the world. I am more awed by those who struggle to make one small difference. ~ Ellen Goodman

I finally figured out the only reason to be alive is to enjoy it. ~ Rita Mae Brown

I don't want life to imitate art. I want life to be art. ~ Carrie Fisher

I invite you to join me on the contemplative path of pluralism, the path of willingness to take risk, to fail it to be touched and transformed by the journey. ~ Judith Simmer-Brown

I do not feel inhibited or bound by what I am. That does not mean that I have never had bad scenes relating to being black and/or a woman, it means that other people's craziness has not managed to make me crazy. ~ Lucille Clifton

I do it for the joy it brings, cause I'm a joyful girl. 'Cause the world owes me nothing, we owe each other the world.
~ Any Difranco

I did the best I could with what I had.
~ Carole Mosley Braun

I can honestly say that I was never affected by the question of the success of an undertaking. If I felt it was the right thing to do, I was for it regardless of the possible outcome. ~ Golda Meir

I believe the second half of one's life is meant to be better than the first half. The first half is finding out how you do it. The second half is enjoying it. ~ Frances Lear

I believe that one of life's greatest risk is never daring to risk. ~ Oprah Winfrey

Getting ahead in a difficult profession requires avid faith in yourself that is why some people with mediocre talent, but with great inner drive, go much further than people with vastly superior talent.
~ Sophia Loren

God gives us our relatives. Thank God we can choose our friends. ~ Ethel Watts Mumford

Family faces are magic mirrors. Looking at people who belong to us, we see the past, present, and future. ~ Gail Lumet Buckley

Flexibility is the key to success – along with mutual respect. ~ Deborah Tannen

Explore the idea of what the language that women speak would really be like if no one were there to correct them.
~ Helene Cixous

Everyone needs to be valued. Everyone has the potential to give something back.
~ Princess Diana

Each person must live their life as a model for others. ~ Rosa Parks

Each person is born with the gift. ~ Jaycie Phelps

Don't compromise yourself. You are all you've got. ~ Janis Joplin

We are not what we know but what we are willing to learn. ~ Mary Catherine Bateson

Turn your wounds into wisdom. ~ Oprah Winfrey

Truth is powerful and it prevails.
~ Sojourner Truth

Too much of a good thing can be
wonderful. ~ Mae West

Too many people let other stand in their
way and don't go back for one more try.
~ Rosabeth Kanter

Don't call me a saint. I don't want to be
dismissed that easily. ~ Dorothy Day

Don't be afraid if things seem difficult in
the beginning. That's only the initial
impression. The important thing is to not
retreat; you have to master yourself.
~ Olga Korbut

Does fashion matter? Always – though not
quite as much after death. ~ Joan Rivers

Do not wait for leaders; do it alone,
person to person. ~ Mother Teresa

Creative minds always have been known
to survive any kind of bad training.
~ Anna Freud

Control the one thing you can: your
attitude. ~ Suzanne de Passe

I am a woman in process. I am just like everybody else. I tried to take every conflict, every experience, and learn from it. Life is never dull. ~ Oprah Winfrey

A wonderful is it that nobody needed to wait as single moment before starting to improve the world. ~ Ann Frank

How many cares one loses when one decides not to be something but to be someone. ~ Coco Chanel

Hope is the thing with feathers/that perches in the soul/and sings the tune without words/and never stops at all. ~ Emily Dickinson

Happiness is not a station you arrive at, but a manner of traveling. ~ Margaret B. Runbeck

Happiness is good health and a bad memory. ~ Ingrid Bergman

Civilization is a method of living in an attitude of equal respect for all people. ~ Jane Addams

Children are apt to live up to what you believe of them. ~ Lady Bird Johnson

Be critical. Women have the right to say: this is surface, this falsifies reality, this degrades. ~ Tillie Olsen

At present, our country needs women's idealism and determination, perhaps more in politics than anywhere else. ~ Shirley Chisholm

As people tried to tell me it was an impossible dream, one of the things that kept coming back to me was, "when has it ever been easy?" ~ Lupe Valdez, First woman sheriff of Dallas County, TX

As long as you keep a person down, some part of you has to be down there to hold them down, so it means you cannot soar as you otherwise might. ~ Marian Anderson

You never find yourself until you face the truth. ~ Pearl Bailey

You must learn to say "no" when something is not right for you.
~ Leontyne Price

You must learn day by day, year by year, to broaden your horizon. The more things you love, the more you are interested in, the more you enjoy, the more you are indignant about, the more you have left when anything happens.
~ Ethel Barrymore

There is a way to look at the past. Don't hide from it. It will not catch you if you don't repeat it. ~ Pearl Bailey

There are well-dressed foolish ideas just as there are well-dressed fools.
~ Diane Ackerman

There are no shortcuts to any place worth going. ~ Beverly Sills

There are two ways of meeting difficulties. You alter the difficulties or you alter yourself to meet them. ~ Phyllis Bottome

The woman who starts the race is not the same woman who finishes the race.
~ Anonymous

The willingness to except responsibility for one's own life as a source from which self-respect springs. ~ Joan Didion

The verb "to love" in Persian is "to have a friend." "I love you" translated literally is "I have you as a friend" and "I don't like you" simply means "I don't have you as a friend." ~ Shusha Guppy

The sign of intelligent people is their ability to control emotions by the application of reason. ~ Marya Mannes

The secret of getting ahead is getting started. ~ Sally Berger

The purpose of morality is to teach you, not to suffer and die, but to enjoy yourself and live. ~ Ayn Rand

The person interested in success has to learn to be a failure as a healthy, inevitable part of the process of getting to the top. ~ Dr. Joyce Brothers

The only safe ship in a storm is leadership. ~ Faye Wattleton

Mediocre idea that generates great enthusiasm will go further than a great idea that inspires no one. ~ Mary Kay Ash

Preparing for a presentation?

Giving a talk is a powerful way for women to get visibility, share knowledge and grow their career. Here are some tips …

1. Start with the end in mind - what is the action or next step people will take after your talk.
2. Outline or mind map your thoughts (mind mapping is great for people like me who are dyslexic and don't always think in a straight line).
3. Start saying parts of your talk out loud - for example when you're driving by yourself
4. Record yourself on your phone - even if it's just audio.
5. Be brave - try video as well.
6. Learn a clean joke. Practice it until it's boring.
7. Looking for a friendly audience to test your talk - pets are great for this.

The naked truth is always better than the best dressed lie. ~ Ann Landers

The most radical revolutionary will become a conservative the day after the revolution. ~ Hanna Arendt

The most common way that people give up their power is by thinking they don't have any. ~ Alice Walker

As I give, I get. ~ Mary McLeod Bethune

America is the greatest country in the world for women to achieve their dreams and for men and women alike to seize the opportunities freedom provides. And our best days are yet to come.
~ Kay Bailey Hutchinson

When she stops conforming to the conventional picture of femininity, she finally began to enjoy being a woman.
~ Betty Friedan

When I go around and speak on campuses, I still don't get young man standing up and saying, "how can I combine career and family?"
~ Gloria Steinem

When one door of happiness closes, another opens; but often we look so long at the closed door that we do not see the one that has opened for us. ~ Helen Keller

Alone, all alone/nobody, but nobody/can make it better but her alone.
~ Maya Angelou

Aerodynamically the bumblebee shouldn't be able to fly, but the bumblebee doesn't know that so it goes on flying anyway.
~ Mary Kay Ash

Adventure is worthwhile in itself.
~ Amelia Earhart

Hey strong, positive self-image is the best possible preparation for success.
~ Dr. Joyce Brothers

A major key to recognizing business opportunities is to see your market with fresh eyes. ~ Edie Weiner

A little bad taste is like a nice dash of paprika. ~ Dorothy Parker

A leader takes people where they want to go... A great leader takes people where they don't necessarily want to go, but thought to be. ~ Rosalynn Carter

A bird doesn't sing because it has an answer, it sings because it has a song. ~ Maya Angelou

The vital, successful people I have met all have one common characteristic. They had a plan. ~ Marilyn Van Derber

Don't ever confuse the two, your life and your work. That's what I have to say. The second is only part of the first. ~ Anna Quindlen

Real life seems to have no plots. ~ Ivy Compton-Burnett

Remember no one can make you feel inferior without your consent. ~ Eleanor Roosevelt

Revolution begins with the self, in the self. ~ Toni Cade Bambara

Roller coaster? It's definitely been a roller coaster, satisfying. At the end of the day these issues are very important so it's worth the ride. ~ Christine Todd Whitman

Giving a presentation? Here are some tips ….

1. Take a DEEP breath before you start. If you're nervous, do some squats before walking in the room.
2. Open your talk with a question - This engages the audience. I often start with "how many of you are extroverts?" Then I jokingly say, "the introverts don't even need to raise their hands."
3. Use slides - This keeps people more focused on your remarks and less likely to be distracted by their phone.
4. Include images not words - Avoid text heavy slides.
5. Recap your talk at the end. Provide some action steps people can do.
6. Include your contact info - even if it's a talk within your organization.
7. Reflect - Congratulations! Public speaking is a huge fear for many. Enjoy the moment. It is especially important women are included.

Security is not the meaning of my life.
Great opportunities are worth the risk.
~ Shirley Hufstedler

Self-pity in its early stages is a snug as a
feather mattress. Only when it hardens
does it become uncomfortable.
~ Maya Angelou

When choosing between two evils, I
always like to try the one I've never tried
before. ~ Mae West

When I dared to be powerful, to use my
strength in the service of my vision, then
it becomes less and less important
whether I am afraid. ~ Audre Lorde

When someone tells me there is only one
way to do things, it always lights a fire
under my butt. My instant reaction is, "I'm
going to prove you wrong!" ~ Picabo
Street

When we talk equal pay for equal work,
women in the workplace are starting to
catch up. If we keep going at the current
rate, we will achieve full equality in about
475 years. I don't know if I can wait that
long. ~ Lya Sorano

When will our consciences growth so tender that we will act to prevent human misery rather than avenge it?
~ Eleanor Roosevelt

When you go out into the world remember: compassion, compassion, compassion. ~ Betty Williams

Where there is great love, there are always miracles. ~ Willa Cather

Who knows what women can be when they are finally free to become themselves. ~ Betty Friedan

Women are not inherently passive or peaceful. We're not inherently anything but human. ~ Robin Morgan

Women share with men the need for personal success, even the taste of power, and no longer are we willing to satisfy those needs through the achievements of surrogates, whether husband, children, or merely role models. ~ Elizabeth Dole

Work is either fun or drudgery. It depends on your attitude. I like fun.
~ Colleen C. Barrett

Yes, I have a doubted. I have wandered off the path. I have been lost. But I always return. ~ Helen Hayes

You are your work. Don't trade the stuff of your life, time, for anything more than dollars. That's a rotten bargain.
~ Rita Mae Brown

You can do one of two things; just shut up, which is something I don't find easy, or learn an awful lot very fast, which is what I've tried to do. ~ Jane Fonda

Expect nothing; live frugally on surprise.
~ Alice Walker

You cannot hope to build a better world without improving the individuals. To that end each of us must work for his own improvement, and at the same time share a general responsibility for all humanity, our particular duty being to aid those to whom we think we can be most useful.
~ Marie Curie

You can't take sides when you know the earth is round. ~ Patricia Sun

You don't learn from the situation where you do something well. You enjoy it and you give yourself credit, but you really don't learn from that. You learn from trial and error, trial and error, all the time.
~ Suzanne Farrell

You grew up the day you have your first real laugh at yourself. ~ Ethel Barrymore

You have to have a dream tour which you were working every single day.
~ Dr. Lorraine Monroe

Kind words can be short and easy to speak, but their echoes are truly endless.
~ Mother Teresa

Kindness always fashionable.
~ Amelia B. Barr

Lasting change is a series of compromises. Compromise is alright as long as your values don't change. ~ Jane Goodall

Lead me not into temptation; I can find away myself. ~ Rita Mae Brown

Let us remember to reach back.
~ Dr. Johnetta Cole

Life appears to me to be too short to be spent nursing animosity or registering wrong. ~ Charlotte Brontë

Life is change. Growth is optional. Choose wisely. ~ Karen Kaiser

Like it's either always a tight-rope or a feather bed. Give me the tight-rope.
~ Edith Wharton

Life is not one straight line. Most of us have to be transplanted, like a tree before we blossom. ~ Louise Nevelson

Life is what we make of it, always has been, always will be. ~ Grandma Moses

You just don't luck into things as much you like to think you do. You build step-by-step, whether it's friendships or opportunities. ~ Barbara Bush

You may have to fight a battle more than once to win it. ~ Margaret Thatcher

You must do the thing with you think you cannot do. ~ Eleanor Roosevelt

Youth is, after all just a moment, but it is moment, the spark that you always carry in your heart. ~ Raisa Gorbachev

You cannot shake hands with a clenched fist. ~ Indira Gandhi

There is no charm equal to tenderness of heart. ~ Jane Austen

You've been criticizing yourself for years and it hasn't worked. Try approving of yourself and see what happens.
~ Louise Hay

Travel is more than the seeing of sights; it is a change that goes on, deep and permanent, in the ideas of living.
~ Miriam Beard

Coming back is the thing that enables you to see how all the dots in your life are connected, how one decision leads you another, how one twist of fate, good or bad, brings you to a door that later takes you to another door, which aided by several detours--long hallways and unforeseen stairwells--eventually puts you in the place you are now." ~ Ann Patchett

About Diane Darling

In order to overcome her fear of public speaking, she took acting and standup comedy classes. That out-of-the-box and strategic mindset has been a contributing factor to her success. She was even the commencement speaker at MIT Charm School (yes there is such a thing).

A pioneer in social networking, McGraw-Hill commissioned Diane Darling to write the definitive book on networking in 2003 (before Facebook or LinkedIn) called The Networking Survival Guide. It went into a 2nd printing just 90 days after the book hit the shelves.

She was an early adopter of LinkedIn (her membership # is 16,418 out of 600 million and counting) and helps organizations leverage the platform to recruit top talent, build their brand, and book of business.

Her books have been translated into nine languages. She says it's weird to write a book but she can't always read it.

Location:

She has lived in the Philippines, Thailand, Colorado, Indiana, Alabama and now in Boston, MA.

Her travels include all seven continents and approximately 60 countries.

Clients include:

In addition to her work in the legal field, she has also spoken for 20th Century Fox, MD Anderson, European Cardiology Society, MIT, Massachusetts General Hospital, Zoho, Harvard Business School, Microsoft, Dell/EMC, Bank of America, Association of Fundraising Professionals, YMCA, American Airlines, London School of Economics, Ross School of Business, Fletcher School of Law & Diplomacy, Junior League, Deloitte, EY, Verizon, Gillette, Department of Defense, State Street, Canadian Government, Pfizer, Sanofi, Biogen, American Cancer Society, Prudential, Fidelity Investments, Merrill Lynch, Bain, Ameriprise, Young President's Organization, Motorola, and many others.

Press:

She has appeared in the Wall Street Journal, International Herald Tribune, San Francisco Chronicle, Boston Globe and MSNBC and NBC Nightly News.

Contact info:

Diane@DianeDarling.com or 617.308.0405

 in/DianeDarling

 DianeDarling

 DianeDarlingSpeaker

 DianeDarlingSpeaker

Special thanks to **Nicola Blakemore.**

My crazy English friend now living in the south of France She helped me get this book out by designing the cover and managing the contents.

She teaches people to paint both in France and online.

painting-holidays-france.com

Front cover photos – top to bottom

1. Ruth Bader Ginsburg - Image from article in The Cut, Jan 7, 2015 by Kate Stoffel
2. Jane Austen - Painting, Source unknown
3. Indira Ghandi - One India
4. Gloria Steinem - Photo from Mayshad Mag
5. Betty Friedan - Image from the Global Merit & Essence Awards Network
6. Margaret Thatcher - Image from her Wikipedia page
7. Shirley Chisholm - Image from the website VDare
8. Elizabeth Cady Stanton - Image from Kids Britannica
9. Oprah Winfrey - Image from Good Reads
10. Anne Frank - Image from a high school book project called Bookstravaganza
11. Toni Morrison - Image from Literal Magazine website, Sept 23, 2013
12. Coco Chanel - Image from the website Time & Note
13. Princess Diana - Image from the Archives of the Women's Political Commission
14. Marie Curie - Image from the website Famous People
15. Lady Bird Johnson - Image from Austin Weekly News, July 18, 2007
16. Billie Holiday - Photo from the website the Allen Ginsberg Project
17. Janis Joplin - Image from FanART.tv

Note about images - best efforts were made to find the original source.

Made in the USA
Columbia, SC
06 April 2019